CH00833070

Sleeping with Stones

SLEEPING
with STONES

Serie Barford

'Te Ara Kanohi (The Pathway of the Eye)' was filmed by Anna Marbrook for Going West (2021). 'The midwife and the cello' was previously published on NZ Poetry Shelf (2020), and in *Titirangi Poets e-zine* #7 (2020). 'If you were a tiputa' was published in *broadsheet: new new zealand poetry* #25 (2020); and 'If you were a tiputa' and 'The midwife and the cello' appeared on David Eggleton's New Zealand Poet Laureate blog for the National Library (2020).

First published 2021

Anahera Press
Tāmaki Makaurau Auckland
Aotearoa New Zealand
www.anahera.co.nz

© Serie Barford, 2021

ISBN 978-0-473-57618-9

Publication is kindly assisted by

ARTS COUNCIL OF NEW ZEALAND TOI AOTEAROA

This book is copyright. Apart from fair dealing for the purpose of private study, research, criticism or review, as permitted under the Copyright Act, no part may be reproduced by any process without the prior permission of the publisher.

Cover design and typesetting: Genie De Wit

Cover image: Serie Barford

Author photo: Self-portrait by Serie Barford

Printed by Ligare Ltd, Auckland

Contents

Autumn

Winter

Dedicated to Alain

E pala maʻa, ʻae lē pala ʻupu.

Stones rot, but not words.

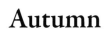

Autumn

Piula blue

I want to return to Piula

swim through the lava tunnel
where we first met

make garlands from laughter
siva with the sun

I want to intercept history
paint DO NOT DISTURB
across your forehead

banish spiteful ghosts
inciting you over the edge

relocate your final standing place
undo your death wish

come my love

follow me down the mountain
through the desert
across the ocean to Piula

fish will lomilomi our tears
into crystalline water

I will kiss you better

The third day

it's the morning of the third day
since I heard you went over the edge

autumn dapples my bewilderment

I arrived at work
was briefed on deadlines
ran away

filled your whisky and wine bottles
with brilliant long-stemmed roses

conjured your smile
pinned it to my pillow

a black dog led you into mountains
past escarpments marked by petroglyphs

I hope ancient birdmen sang a threnody

accompanied your lonely swan dive

If you were a tiputa

if you were a tiputa
I'd steal you from the museum

treat and preserve you

lift soil from your shoulders
with low-pressure suction

divert the landslide
that swept you away

swab you with blotting paper
parcelled in acid-free tissues

bathe you like a delicate artefact

lay you in humidification chambers
rehydrate your brittle parts

tenderly lacquer your frayed edges
patch gaping wounds with kozo

drape you over my shoulders
slumber within your barkcloth folds

press you against my heart

Sleeping with stones

people skirt my grief
avoid me

don't be afraid
I'm not a fish hook

warmly hug

release me

I'll swim again

please say his name
don't double-dead him

visit when the sun is high
the kettle boiling
the horizon is eating the sun

we can ransack the fridge
drink bottomless glasses

laugh
cry
laugh

and when everyone has gone

I'll fasten the rickety gate

slide between sheets warmed by stones
each one a memory of a day well spent

peck comfort like a hungry bird

rock myself to sleep

Eating flowers

Jojo arrives in her four-wheel drive
gripping kai from the bakery

pours the kettle
arranges pizza slices like flowers

I move my lips
teeth follow them

this how I chew

stay alive

Frogmarch

it's the evening of the fifth day
since I heard you went over the edge

the phone rings
a voice asks how I'm doing

I'm watching film clips of the waterfall
studying rocks from different angles
calculating the trajectory of his fall
the volume of water
the force of its magnificence
the magnitude of his pain

wondering if I was his last thought

imagining cold shock response
silencing his Leo roar

the voice tells me it's time to move on

I smash the phone against the wall

the voice should know better
than to frogmarch grief

Losing balance

predators gnawed holdfasts
undermined your standing place

unanchored

you ricocheted through wastelands
my fagameme'i couldn't bring you down

sickness changed your scent

the salty lick of sunshine and ocean
infused with alofa

oxidised
soured

we slept without spooning

I dreamed of harmonic keys
unlocking peace
balance

they hovered between

us

Pick one I whispered

your eyes narrowed
They're after me!

Under siege

you slept alert
hands ready to strangle

frisked me for grenades

evaded doctors
priests
healers

I hid the knife block

wept

my lover turned foe

you switched
plates at dinner

made me taste
your food

for poison

What remains

you had a neck built for scrums
shoulders strong for heavy loads
.fingers like sea anemones

my towering neck is scarred

people make assumptions

you shouldn't apply perfume
then sleep in the sun

you shouldn't argue with drunks
butting out cigarettes

you shouldn't lie in grass
trampled by hedgehogs

you shouldn't cut pain
from uncovered body parts

you shouldn't touch handrails
in public places

you shouldn't scratch
with unwashed hands

you shouldn't drive
without a seat belt

you shouldn't cuddle animals
that don't belong to you

you shouldn't bleach your skin
you're too bloody pale already

you tried strangling the scars away
they wouldn't budge

I use concealer to dull their brightness

whiten my teeth

smile

Protection

ancestors stationed bodyguards
brandished claymore and sharktooth clubs

you retreated to the sofa

larvaé breeding fear and hate
festered inside your head

you made choices
packed up
left

I loved you
still do

can't imagine opening to anyone else

friends say
Give yourself time

Connections

Fatumea was renamed 'Piula' by Methodists
after Beulah who was married to the Lord

you'd followed celestial bodies to Piula
I'd followed family

it was the cyclone season

my uncle's friend was steaming in a taxi
with a woman who wasn't his wife

you were a familiar stranger
with an accent I couldn't place

entered
left my life

via a pool of water

Cyclone

your thoughts stirred a tempest
all the ingredients were there

heat
moisture
instability
pressure

you frantically drummed your head

listened for soft spots
a release valve

but fontanelles that once slipped
like tectonic plates
had set into a pinnacled crust

you howled into a Category 5

fell from the sky

raged over water

struck rocks

Becoming the sky

I imagine you falling
head first into the abyss

tumbling

tumbling

tumbling

hokohoko shirt billowing

ego's shroud unbuttoning
pulling free
ascending

slicing blue
at the foot of the falls

heart exploding

becoming the sky

Winter

Comfort food

grief has fangs
an insatiable appetite

my mother tries to help

feeds me pisupo
palusami
pai apa

weeds herbs she doesn't recognise

when I go for thyme
it has already gone

Too close for comfort

Kia ora

about that mammogram

I'm cancelling the appointment
my breasts are too close to my heart

if they're squeezed between glass plates
I'll shatter

Kia ora

Water songs

pigeons flock to our fale at sunrise

I scatter birdseed
scoop water from bowls

tilt my palms so it trickles
tinkles
splashes
sings to thirsty birds

pigeons are suction drinkers
draw moisture into hollow bones

I pour coffee for one
lurch through days
hunker in your chair at night

Masina rises full and luscious
sings recalcitrant tides into kings

I pour nightcaps

wonder which song lured you over the falls
if there were sirens in your head

The dark side of the moon

grief is a fist of whirling mussel shells
slicing
scraping
shredding what remains

a white pigeon heard you'd flown the coop
took me gently under his wing

Filemu Filemu Filemu I crooned
offered water
seeds
leftovers

he ate everything except cooked carrots

was a peaceful presence in my dismantled world

one morning Filemu was gone
waning Masina rested instead
on the guano-splattered roof

I ached to patch her incomplete beauty

I am fully present Masina chided. *Heal yourself
instead of tinkering with my perfection.*

I closed my eyes

saw the dark side of the moon

white feathers falling like rain

Sprinkling water to restore life

I heard high-pitched squeals
imagined a bird in distress

rushed over slippery bridges
into grass heavily rutted by tyres

equine necks straining a wire fence
alerted me to tragedy

a hedgehog newly drowned in mud
beneath their sorrowful gaze

I tried to resurrect the warm stillness

couldn't

there was a note in your backpack
Do not reanimate me
written in three languages

Pacific warriors were restored to life
with water from sacred springs

you fought black dogs for decades
chose the pool of no return

moe le toa
let the warrior sleep

Fate

you were already a father
before I'd kissed my first love

who would've thought we'd meet

a syncretic woman from the south
a medicine man from the north

at Piula

Finding your eyes

Matariki has risen
night's eyes are plentiful

but where are yours?

did they settle in fissures
float down rivers to the sea?

were they found by children
played as marbles
eaten by piranhas?

did they fly from your head
smash like snails on rocks
rot beneath the sun?

every night I lie in bed
beside your photo

stare out the window

search for a familiar twinkle

What I found

I found a DO NOT FOLD OR BEND! x-ray
tucked behind pillows in our wardrobe

gently tugged you from an envelope

torso intact
a snapshot of a healthy man

asymmetrical birds flew into my hands

your lungs
fully inflated

caged in ribs
shining like polished shells

it's the longest night of the year

I'm lying in darkness
clutching your silhouette

heart to heart
percussive beats echo

you dance within my arms

What we harvest

you sculled drinks
sailed boats
scaled octaves
climbed mountains
like a man accustomed to altitude

joyfully plumbed my slippery depths
as if freediving for pearls

licked garlic butter from bread
fumigated me with searing kisses

it's the winter solstice

time to break garlic bulbs into cloves
bury them in Papatūānuku to incubate
make more of themselves

garlic juice is an adhesive
mends porcelain and glass

if I sew garlic in your grave
will your bones caulk

sail again?

Te Ara Kanohi (The Pathway of the Eye)

our favourite coastal walk
took us over rivers
past grazing horses

onto a track of expansive views
marked by orange stakes
pegging headlands to the surf

you were an adventurer
a doctor of medicine
a specialist of bones

treated unsettled thoughts
as mischievous strangers
best drunk into oblivion
then shown the door

last time we trod this path
you were swaying

clutching your heart
grieving Sirius
our dog

like light-demanding whau
you sank beneath the weight
of too many shadows

but Sirius rose again
shines brightly in his star kennel

Spring

What we carry

I never asked when you'd return
you always flew home

no words needed
just trust

once you arrived in spring
crumpled and stubbled

we embraced
drank aperitifs in the garden

a shining cuckoo trilled

we marvelled at the bird's endurance
how it clutches a white pebble during flight
licks the cool surface to ward off thirst

you proposed a toast
To spring and safe returns!

we laughed
drank from each other's glasses

my best friend
my migratory bird
my love

Heartbeat

the sun's melody is a deep throb
the heartbeat of our universe

solar storms gallop in all directions

o fea le alofa?
where is love?

I wish

I wish I'd anchored you with rocks
in a lagoon fenced by coral

watched fish devour your hectic thoughts
the ocean launder a lifetime of pain

hooked you with my thumb
raised you to greet the sun

gently cocooned the reborn you
giddy with the lightness of being

told you how much I love you
not that I fear for my life

when you cut bread
my eyes reflected your face

I wish I'd followed star maps

extended my palm toward the horizon
like a wayfarer squaring constellations

let the one-degree width of my pinkie
tickle your funny bone coordinates

plotted your location

put my finger on the second
your lights went out

recalibrated your course

sailed with you into a new dawn

Rhumb line

we met decades ago

you were travelling light
hand luggage only

so it seemed

followed me home
wanted in
eventually wanted out

we're connected by tusili'i

I'll cast a rhumb line
ride it over swell
skim mountains and clouds
ricochet off zenith stars

until I reach the mythical shore
where you are strands of glistening light
the sequel to a storm

a rainbow

Blue birds

I found a nest tumbled by wind
into a mangrove forest

one cracked blue egg
slightly dewy
lolled above the tide

a woman stopped to stare

Two nests blew from tōtara
onto my back yard

there was so much blue

the eggs
pieces of plastic
thread woven with twigs

birds know blue she said

I nodded

flew away

What if

kōwhai in full throttle
fringe rivers feeding the dam

golden bells float the wind
cascade waterfalls
peal over spillways
punctuate water with radiance

what if you'd slipped into this dam
been filtered and treated

pumped out fit for purpose
continued your business of living

we'd be revelling in spring
the bobbing poi of ecstatic tūī

joyfully harmonising
with messengers of the gods

Photoshoot

the radiographer is professionally pleasant
but my breasts have minds of their own

they slip-sag-slide off the apparatus
jiggle into their customary horizon

the radiographer nudges my waist
Relax. Drop your shoulders.

repositions my left breast
gently turns my chin
tilts my hip
lowers the compression paddle

I'm pinned in loveless intimacy
in a drab room on an empty stomach

the radiographer stands behind her shield
activates the photo shoot

x-rays spurt through flesh
expose everything
flood chambers you still inhabit

it's the first time I've been touched
since you went over the edge

tears and snot smudge machinery

I apologise
scramble into clothes

it's not easy my love
yesteryear is as close as yesterday

but right now
I'm eating mangoes

smiling at photos of dogs
swimming with feral pigs

squealing delight

I see you

you're an intrepid traveller

border controls
police reports
a death certificate
a grave
won't pin you down

mist morphs into your figure

we wave through organza curtains
blow kisses

Summer

Imprints

our pōhutukawa grows strongly
with memories of your touch

bloomed early this summer
snares the neighbour's sun

you rang from a whare for whirlwind minds
asked about trees you'd never see again

said you missed me
cried

There's too many ghosts here
they piss on me when I sleep!

doctors scoffed but I believed you
that whare has wartime history

eugenics and mass murder
test subjects for pharmaceuticals

souls stymied by trauma
disturb the unsettled

there's so little of you left for me to clutch
when days run like truculent oil slicks

when I'm slipping
falling
breaking

so I hug our tree
nuzzle its crimson blooms

Roots

you broke suburban rules

planted saplings above water pipes
ignored sprinkler restrictions during a drought

staked mānuka and kānuka
beneath saggy powerlines

How do I know which is which?

Kind kānuka I said
stroking the soft leaves

mean mānuka
deliberately pricking your palms

They'll entangle the lines I warned

you just laughed
washed your hands
cracked open a beer

I plotted a replant but you got sick

said you needed your own tribe
the spine of ancestral mountains
the comfort of your mother tongue
your village pub and friends

we agreed to separate lives

you nestled into distant roots to heal
realised too late they were here

I really thought we'd meet again
but one afternoon you turned arborist

topped yourself

Sing to me

daisies push themselves up
I lop off their heads

can barely mow the lawn
their wailing disturbs me

your fine voice lies buried
on the other side of the world

how you loved our garden

pese mai
sing to me

Summer equinox

I'm scribing banana leaves with permanent ink
stick figures and pithy messages for you

curved fingers of fruit sweetly point up
how I miss your body!

everything has its season
suckers wriggle in anticipation

today is the longest day of the year

I'm imagining your smile
an unfurling wave

flick eyebrows into the sun
absorb radiation so you can track me

through solitude

Survival

I arrived at the medical centre

encountered a herd of elephants
grazing on high plastered walls

the matriarch noted my astonishment

swished her tail
gently rumbled

nudged me toward reception

the tapping fingers of a nurse
bored by wildlife documentaries

he gave me a kimono
whispered *Leave your panties on*

fitted earplugs
fed me into a cavernous machine
where I lay dead-still for an hour

rose again

heard shouting
gunfire
trumpets

ran to the waiting room

found the herd huddled behind couches
mourning an aunty slain by poachers

bowed before the matriarch
Aroha mai. My kind is so cruel.

she clasped me with her trunk
showed me the door

My graffitied heart

I am a calabash
a palette of stardust
a walking river
an island
a dreamer
a graffitied heart

I have weathered
winter's frigid persistence
cyclones
earthquakes
heat waves
landslides
droughts
tsunamis
depression

I have tackled credit cards
banished villains
decluttered houses
repaired cars with super glue

eaten eggs for breakfast
oysters for lunch
ambrosia for dessert

loved and lost
raised children
fallen apart

terrorised my limping shadow

tunnelled deep to meet grief
kanohi ki te kanohi

found compassion

excavated air pockets
struck bedrock
melted into this planet's core
run with lava to the sea

toasted your birthday
danced to Django Reinhardt

survived a parabolic fall

regained my footing

kept walking

Geometries of light

when I was small I watched clouds
morph into phantasmagorical creatures

flit crazily over houses
piss on unsuspecting hills

dislodged sticky beads from paspalum
flicked them at thieving ants

pressed thumbs against reclining lids
until retinas exploded into phosphenes

blue stars
kaleidoscopes
fireworks

banished the bogeyman

I wish you'd played this game darl
activated geometries of light

welded the frayed end of your tether

Into the world of light

I resolutely lanced my heart
a swollen fist about to burst

with a shark tooth plucked from a dream

poured honey into the first chamber

soothed gnawed memories
sent them west with wild bees

insulated the second chamber with foliage

kawakawa hearts blanketed loss
tempered feelings of abandonment

painted the third chamber gold

ground turmeric mixed with coconut oil
loosened inflammation's angry grip

poulticed the fourth chamber with suka

toxins drawn into a sweet citadel
dissolved into spontaneous sun showers

bandaged myself with banana leaves
waded into the ocean

the shark tooth pulsed
warned off predators

suspended beyond the measure of clocks

floating

floating

floating

until my grandmother's kingfisher brought me ashore

embraced by pouliuli

my ruptured casement of grief
flew into the world of light

The midwife and the cello

I was perched amongst pīngao
contemplating a paragliding instruction

Don't look at what you want to miss

when a woman sat beside me

pointed at the lagoon's mouth
breaking into hazardous surf

crooned *I'm a midwife*
sing and play cello

I observed her eloquent hands
iron sand burying sprawling feet
lines networking a benevolent smile
dreads tied with frayed strips of cotton

remembered you returning home
buoyant with the miracle of birth

the baby with omniscient eyes
you eased into this world

how she lay within your arms

didn't cry

Moving on

my breasts won't pertly tilt
into last season's foam-cupped sunfrock

they've succumbed to gravitational pull

slide beneath the youthful bodice
bulge where material should lie flat

I'm not sure you'd recognise me in the dark

I bought the frock on sale
(you'd like that)

it's summer-sky blue

A matter of time

the living sing
so do the dead

I should know
my dreams are operas

a phantom lali
beats time

a countdown

we will be together again

hand on heart

promise

Notes

Piula Cave Pool   a natural freshwater pool by the sea
beneath the Methodist chapel at Piula,
north coast of Upolu island, Sāmoa

siva   (Samoan) dance

lomilomi   (Samoan) type of massage

tiputa   poncho-like garments made from
barkcloth. The processes described
in the poem are from the 2017 paper
'Re-evaluating student treatments of
barkcloth artefacts from the Economic
Botany Collection, Royal Botanic
Gardens, Kew', by Mark Nesbitt, Misa
Tamura and Frances Lennard.

kozo   (Japanese) paper made from the paper
mulberry bush, commonly used in
conservation and repair work

double-dead   the first death is when a person physically
dies, the second when a person is no
longer remembered

kai   (Māori) food

alofa   (Samoan) love

fagameme'i   (Samoan) slingshot

hokohoko	(Māori) to trade, barter, sell; often used in relation to second-hand shops/items
pisupo	(Samoan) canned corn beef
palusami	(Samoan) coconut cream wrapped in taro leaves, cooked in umu/ground oven
pai apa	(Samoan) pineapple pie
kia ora	(Māori) a greeting wishing good health
Masina	(Samoan) Moon, personification of the moon. When lowercase, also means 'month'.
Papatūānuku	(Māori) Mother Earth
Filemu	(Samoan) peace, quiet, stillness. Also a reference to Black Saturday in 1929, when independence leader Tupua Tamasese Lealofi III, dressed in white, called out 'Filemu, filemu, peace peace', but was fatally shot by New Zealand police.
Matariki	(Māori) the Pleiades or Seven Sisters; also the brightest star of that cluster. The rise of Matariki signals the beginning of the new year for many Māori tribes.
Te Ara Kanohi	(Māori) The Pathway of the Eye
whau	(Māori) a small tree of Aotearoa New Zealand also known as corkwood

Sirius	the Dog Star, one of the brightest stars in the sky. Also name of author's deceased dog.
rhumb line	a curve on the surface of a sphere that cuts all meridians at the same angle; the path taken by a vessel that maintains a constant compass direction
tusiliʻi	(Samoan) fine or wavy lines used to connect individual designs and spaces on siapo/tapa cloth
tōtara	(Māori) a forest canopy tree of Aotearoa New Zealand valued for building waka/ canoes and for carving
kōwhai	(Māori) a flowering tree of Aotearoa New Zealand with bright yellow blossoms
poi	(Māori) a style of performing art; a tethered swinging weight used by performers; the white throat tufts of a tūī
tūī	(Māori) a songbird from Aotearoa New Zealand with a white throat tuft and two voice boxes
whare	(Māori) house
aroha mai	(Māori) older translation is 'forgive me' or 'be compassionate to me', now often used to mean 'I'm sorry' or 'my apologies'

kanohi ki te kanohi (Māori) face to face

Django Reinhardt Belgian-born Romani-French jazz
guitarist (1910–1953), regarded as one
of the greatest musicians of the twentieth
century

fale (Samoan) house

paspalum a perennial grass, weed

phosphenes luminous images produced by the
stimulation of the retina, such as by
pressure applied to the eyeball when the
eye is closed

kawakawa (Māori) a widely used plant of Aotearoa
New Zealand with green, heart-shaped
leaves

suka (Samoan) sugar

pouliuli (Samoan) dark night, blackness, void

pīngao (Māori) golden sand sedge, once
common on sand dunes throughout
Aotearoa New Zealand, used by weavers
for patterning highlights

lali (Samoan) a large drum made of a
hollowed log